A Devoted Family's Journey

Our Daughter's Battle against a Brain Tumor

FELICIA *and* CHARLES WILLIAMS

A DEVOTED FAMILY'S JOURNEY
OUR DAUGHTER'S BATTLE AGAINST A BRAIN TUMOR

iUniverse books may be ordered through booksellers or by contacting:

iUniverse
1663 Liberty Drive
Bloomington, IN 47403
www.iuniverse.com
844-349-9409

Because of the dynamic nature of the internet, any web addresses or links contained in this book may have changed since publication and may no longer be valid. The views expressed in this work are solely those of the author and do not necessarily reflect the views of the publisher, and the publisher hereby disclaims any responsibility for them.

Any people depicted in stock imagery provided by Getty Images are models, and such images are being used for illustrative purposes only. Certain stock imagery © Getty Images.

ISBN: 978-1-6632-1614-4 (sc)
ISBN: 978-1-6632-1615-1 (e)

Library of Congress Control Number: 2021900477

Print information available on the last page.

iUniverse rev. date: 04/14/2021

This book is dedicated to our daughter Kariina. She has fought so hard from day one of her journey and through this whole process. You truly are an amazing, strong girl that deserves the world. Mommy and Daddy are so proud of you every day.

Special thanks to everyone who was involved and helped us get through this journey of our life. You know who you are!

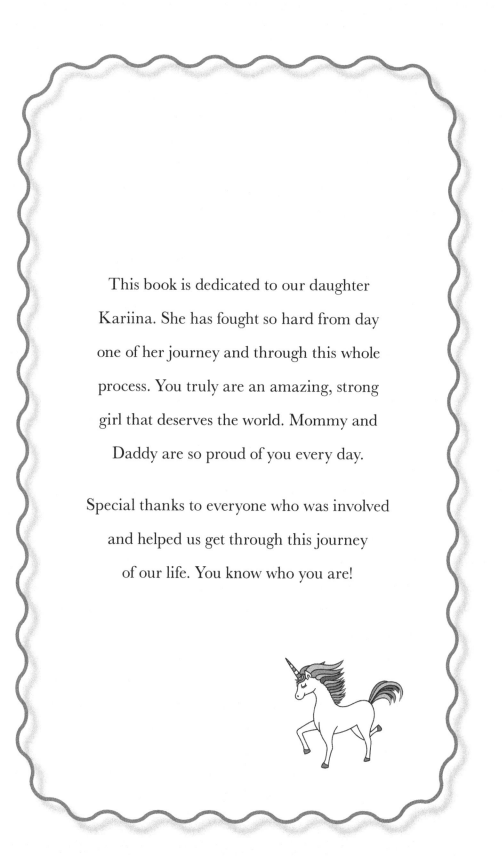

It was a cold Monday when I realized something was wrong. My eight-year-old daughter had been complaining about headaches for almost three months. She constantly needed Tylenol to keep the pain at bay. She would sleep anywhere from twelve to fourteen hours a day if I let her.

I knew in my heart something was truly wrong. As a mother, I just didn't want to face it. I went through a checklist: could it be allergies, a sinus infection, a change in her vision? Two different doctors had sent us away with antibiotic regimens. She still did not seem to be getting any better. She was seen by an eye doctor. The doctor said, "Her vision has not changed at all."

She was involved in soccer, basketball, and gymnastics at the time. So I thought she was just burned out from all her activities and schoolwork. She was an amazing

student and always tried her best in everything she did. She had a lot of friends and was a social butterfly.

I had gradually seen a lot of those things change. She had gone from being social to not caring who was around her. She had always wanted to be active, but then she started wanting to sleep all the time. In sports, her coordination slowly declined. Especially noticeable was a lack of balance, which led to several falls. Her headaches got worse and worse. She couldn't even tolerate a loud assembly at school. Luckily for me, I worked at her school and was able to check in on her from time to time.

It all hit on a cold January morning. It was January 14, 2019, a day our family would never forget. She woke up with a major headache, and I told her to take a warm shower to see if that would help. As soon as she stepped out of the shower, she vomited all over the floor. I knew it was time to get more answers. I was determined to demand an x-ray at any cost. There was something truly wrong.

Her doctor's office got her in that same morning. It was a different doctor than the one who usually saw her because her regular pediatrician happened to be on vacation. I urgently explained to the new doctor that there was something truly wrong. I needed answers!

He said, "I think it's just a sinus infection. Maybe a stronger antibiotic is needed."

I replied, "I know my instincts, and I don't think this is a sinus infection."

The doctor paused for about five seconds. Then he looked up at me. "A mother's intuition is usually a thing. I'll call the hospital to request a CT scan for her."

We left the doctor's office and headed to the hospital, where they did the CT scan. Afterward, the x-ray technician said, "Please head to the waiting room. I'm going to see if the pediatrician would like any other tests performed while you're here."

After forty-five minutes of waiting, I went up and asked the receptionist if we could go home since we had waited so long. The receptionist said, "They are still waiting on the doctor to make a decision."

I sat down again. Things got tense. Between my daughter's condition and not knowing any specifics, my level of stress was at an all-time high.

Finally, the receptionist came to get us. She said, "The doctor is here to see you guys."

My heart dropped with worry. The thoughts running through my head were *Why would this doctor travel fifteen minutes to the hospital to see us? Is this a protocol? Is something wrong?*

A nurse came and said, "I will take your daughter into another room to play while you talk to the doctor." At that point I knew something wasn't right.

I walked into the room where the doctor was waiting. My heart felt like it fell out of my chest when I saw the look on his face. I asked, "Why are you here? Is everything OK with my daughter?"

He looked me in the eye and said, "You definitely

had a mother's intuition when you felt something wasn't right. There is a golf ball–size tumor in your daughter's cerebellum, at the back of her brain."

I started to cry. "What needs to be done? How could this have happened? She is only eight years old! She has so much life to live!" I could not imagine explaining this to her, my husband, my five-year-old son, or my one-year-old daughter. How could this happen to our family?

The pediatrician didn't have many answers. This was a rare thing to happen to an eight-year-old. He recommended we go to Riley Hospital for Children that same day to talk with a neurosurgeon. A specialist could explain our options and perform advanced imaging. The pediatrician had already contacted the team at Riley, and they were awaiting our arrival.

I had so many questions. Would we have to stay the night there? Was this a quick appointment? What about the family's schedule? I had a job, my husband had a job, my son was in school, and my little one was in day care.

My life wasn't ready for any of this. My husband and I had just gotten married. We'd never even had the chance to have a honeymoon. We were possibly going to have to stay at the hospital as if it were a five-star resort.

But this appointment was our main priority, given that my daughter's overall health was clearly declining. We decided my husband would stay home with the two younger kids, and the two of us explained the situation to the whole family.

After a lot of tears and asking why and how, my daughter and I drove three dreadful hours to Indianapolis. We arrived at the emergency room of Riley Hospital for Children, where they were indeed waiting for us.

We saw several doctors and nurses, beginning with a neurosurgeon. My daughter was sent for a three-and-a-half-hour MRI. Halfway through, she went into anaphylactic shock because she was allergic to the contrast media they put in through her IV. They had to pause the MRI and rush her back to the emergency room for medication to calm things down so they could finish the MRI.

Once the MRI was complete, we again went to the emergency room. Things were really low for us at that point. She was experiencing back-to-back issues that worried us.

The neurosurgeon came back and said, "I am going to consult with my whole team and come up with the best plan for your daughter. Due to the size of the tumor and the amount of fluid surrounding it, I want to admit her this evening. We'll start her on a steroid to reduce the inflammation and discuss more options in the morning."

We were hurt by the news. It was hard to sleep, thinking about things that would have to be done to a child so young and innocent.

My daughter was admitted to the intensive care unit at Riley, where she was closely monitored by an ICU nurse all day and all night. We became close with one of the nurses who cared for her in the days leading up to her surgery. The nurse really had a great relationship with our daughter and kept her feeling positive.

The next afternoon—January 15, 2019—two neurosurgeons entered my daughter's room. One was the doctor who had met with us in the emergency room. The other was the one who was going to change our lives. He was the one who was going to operate on my little girl.

The surgeon pulled up her MRI images and discussed what we were seeing and what would be the best-case scenario for her. He said that, based on the size and location of the tumor, it could be any of three different types. He wouldn't know which type it was until it was removed and biopsied. He then said, "I would like to keep her on the steroid for a couple of days to reduce the amount of fluid around the tumor. That will help it come out more easily."

This made sense to me but was also frustrating. I thought about my husband and two children three hours away. I didn't know the next time I would be able to see them. What was going to happen with only me here for my daughter? I was trying to be the strongest person I could possibly be for her, but I was terrified. I didn't know what was going to happen.

The neurosurgeons advised me to have my husband come before the surgery. Their opinion was I shouldn't be alone for such a big day. My husband arrived that evening after work. The hospital staff was nice enough to call a Ronald McDonald House to see if we could stay there since we didn't know how long we would be staying in Indianapolis.

At first we were told it could be a couple of days before we would get a room, due to limited capacity. We decided to wait until we knew if we could get a room before we got our other two kids. Luckily for us, we got a call at 6:30 that evening. A room had opened up.

My husband and I stayed there that night. I then left early the next morning to pack up our belongings and pick up our other children. It felt like an eternity since I had seen them, but it had only been two days. Of course, they had many questions for me. But they were very little, so I wanted to save them a little sanity and emotion. I also wanted them to see how their sister was before her surgery the next day.

My husband and I still could not believe this was going on. Things had certainly taken a wrong turn. We didn't realize that we were too early in the process to perceive it all. No one could tell us anything at that point because they didn't know. No one knew how long we would be away from our everyday lives, school, and jobs.

Once the kids and I got back to Indianapolis, we had a brief hi-and-bye with the whole family, and then it was time for bed. We made sure to get our daughter whatever she wanted to eat before bed. She asked for a Hardee's chicken tender meal, but she had absolutely no appetite. She was getting sicker by the day. We knew it was time for her to get better. You have to do what's best for your child, and we felt like the surgery would save her life.

The next morning, January 17, 2019, was her big surgery. We hoped it would go smoothly and we would be discharged from the hospital the next day. My husband and I didn't sleep all night. We were sick to our stomachs, thinking about our little girl having to go through such an intense surgery.

It was time to say our goodbyes and stay positive for her. I could tell how nervous she was as the nurse and anesthesiologist rolled her back to the operating room. I started crying; so did she. Then she looked up at me and said, "Mom, I got this. It will be fine."

The surgery lasted ten and a half hours, and through it all we got constant updates from an operating room nurse. Finally, we got a call that the neurosurgeon was ready to talk to us about how her surgery went. He explained the tumor had been fully removed, but it was cancerous and stage 4. The tumor type was a medulloblastoma.

He told us that my daughter would need about six

weeks to recover from the surgery. During this time, she would be getting various kinds of therapy: physical (PT), occupational (OT), speech, and respiratory. Next, she would have six weeks of proton radiation, and then seven months of chemotherapy. This was to make sure the tumor didn't return.

We were also informed that she had a small tube coming out of her head, called an EVD. It monitored the amount of fluid coming out of her brain and showed the doctors whether she could tolerate having a device called a shunt. A shunt drains cerebral fluid regularly so that it doesn't fill the skull and enlarge the brain. We spent many sleepless nights checking on it and making sure things were good on the monitors. It was literally a full-time job.

Imagine our situation. Where do you start to ask questions? My husband and I cried and cried. We were newlyweds, ready to start a new chapter in our lives.

How was this happening? The not-knowing was so difficult for us.

After the conversation with the neurosurgeon, we wanted to see our daughter. He informed us it might be two hours before we were allowed to see her because she had to awaken from the anesthesia. My husband left to get our other two children, who at the time were being cared for by my cousin. She had been nice enough to make the trip so my husband and I could be together during my daughter's surgery.

There was another wait before a nurse called me back to my daughter's room. It had been a total of twelve and a half hours since I saw her rolling into surgery. The nurse said she should have woken up by then, but she hadn't. I was terrified. The worst part about it was that my husband wasn't there with me. I waited up all night to see if she would awaken, and she still did not.

It was almost a whole day before she opened her eyes. The doctors said this wasn't a normal thing. Many thoughts were going through my head. This possibility hadn't been explained to us prior to the operation.

My daughter finally woke up. The news still was not good. The doctors explained that she was unable to move any part of her body. She couldn't talk, use the bathroom, or even eat normal food. We decided to have the nurses put a tube through her nose, to give her the nutrients she needed to survive until she was able to eat. Life seemed upside down.

The doctors informed us that my daughter's condition was called cerebellum mutism and posterior fossa syndrome. Researching that was a scary, intimidating thing. Our main focus was on getting our daughter healthier so she could withstand the next two phases she had to undergo.

Meanwhile, the rest of the family went back and forth from the hospital to the Ronald McDonald House, waiting for my daughter's condition to normalize. It was odd not being able to eat our own cooked meals;

we survived on food the Ronald McDonald House occasionally provided and on eating out. Little did we know her recovery wouldn't be a quick process.

The brain is one of the biggest organs in the human body and one of the most powerful. The brain controls the whole body. During the first week of our stay at Riley Hospital for Children, my daughter was in the PICU (pediatric intensive care unit). In the second week, she was transferred to the neuro unit for three weeks. There, they told us the EVD could come out of her head. They decided she did not need a shunt because her brain was able to withstand the pressure of the fluid on its own, without needing a device. We were thrilled.

The doctors did invasive testing to see what subtype of medulloblastoma her tumor was. There are four possible subtypes. We were happy to learn she had a WNT positive tumor, which meant she could have less chemotherapy and radiation—a good thing for her prognosis. Less was better for her overall recovery.

The last two weeks we spent in the inpatient rehabilitation unit. During this time, our son had a tutor who helped him keep up with school since we had to pull him out for three months. She was amazing. She contacted his teacher at home and got work from her so he wouldn't be behind at all when he went back to school.

Meanwhile, our daughter was getting PT, OT, speech therapy, and respiratory therapy. During week 5 of her recovery, the therapists did a swallow study to assess whether she could eat solid food again. She was able to eat thickened liquids, which lasted for a couple of weeks until swallowing got easier and stronger for her. Then she graduated to a normal diet. The first food she wanted was chicken alfredo from Olive Garden and lobster from Red Lobster. We would have done anything at that point to make her happy.

My husband and I had to explain to her what the next phase of treatment would be after leaving the children's hospital. It was terrible telling my eight-year-old what she was about to go through, and she couldn't move or speak to tell us how she felt. She was completely the same person inside. She was so frustrated that she would cry. As a parent, I just couldn't hold it together. I cried all day and night. I just didn't understand why someone had done this to our family and my baby.

After six long weeks at the children's hospital, we were off to Illinois for another six weeks at a different Ronald McDonald House. My daughter had to stay in another inpatient rehabilitation hospital while undergoing six more dreadful weeks of proton radiation. We shuttled between the Ronald McDonald House, Marianjoy Rehabilitation Hospital, and the outpatient Northwestern Medicine Proton Center. The Ronald McDonald House was beautiful, and the people we met there made our stay feel like home.

Even so, at times it really felt like more than we had bargained for. My husband and I switched off to be either with our sick daughter or at the Ronald McDonald

House with our other two children. We tried to keep them happy, but all they wanted to do was go home. This was extremely stressful and took a toll on my husband's and my relationship.

The rehab hospital had some great therapists, but the nurses were not the best. One nurse went above and beyond to make sure we were as comfortable as possible; she was truly a blessing. Most of them just wanted to shove meds down my daughter's throat. However, the doctor there was amazing and was willing to try anything to help our daughter get better.

The proton center personnel made an awful situation as positive as they could. When my daughter started to eat more, they would bring her McDonald's breakfast hash browns and donuts from Dunkin Donuts. They really tried hard to make her feel special.

During this horrific time, she lost all her beautiful, curly hair. While going through radiation, she slowly got her speech back and was able to move her legs and arms again. She still wasn't walking, but she was able to sit on her own by the end of our stay. She was also strong enough to start doing schoolwork again. That was an important plus because she had missed three months of school at that point.

Things progressed, but not fast enough for us to resume our busy lifestyle at home. At the end of proton therapy, we were excited to say goodbye and go back to our home. Three months away from one's own home is absolutely horrific. I never wanted to leave my home again.

The two-and-a-half-hour drive felt like the best drive possible. The house felt brand-new to us. We arrived to a clean house—family members had helped make sure we had no work to do. We also were fortunate to have a family member build a ramp and deck in our backyard. Our daughter couldn't walk up stairs to get in and out of the house.

We enjoyed being home together for a couple of days.

Then it was time for my husband to go back to work and my son to go back to school. I had to find an outpatient rehabilitation center for my daughter because she still needed PT, OT, and speech therapy services. After I called several places, I found one that would take her two days a week for PT and OT. It took more time to find a speech therapist; most speech therapists have long wait lists. We were fortunate to find an amazing speech therapist who would work with our schedule.

The following week, we met our local oncologist at Beacon Children's Hospital. This doctor worked with my daughter for the next seven months. She continued my daughter's chemotherapy. She was amazing, the best around. She worked remotely with the team we first started with at Riley Hospital for Children. She managed the whole chemotherapy schedule and regimen of medications my daughter needed to feel better. She was thorough and didn't miss anything. To this day, we are thrilled to see her because she has done everything possible to bring our daughter safely through a gruesome process.

For a while, we went continuously back and forth to the hospital, sometimes staying three nights at a time. Other times, it was just a quick six-hour visit for outpatient chemotherapy.

On December 20, 2019, my daughter received her last dose of vincristine. We couldn't have been any more thrilled to know that we were coming to the end of this brutal journey. They did a great job at the hospital making the day special for our daughter. She received bags filled with presents for Christmas. It really made her day.

We still had a long recovery ahead, but medically she was flourishing again. In October 2020, we decided to switch to a new therapy center, where they specialized in treating children with neurological conditions. The center is amazing and to this day continues to work my daughter extremely hard. When she first got there, she could barely walk with a walker; she was mostly in a wheelchair. We thank everyone there for helping with her progress. She is forever grateful, as are my husband and I, to have such a dedicated team of therapists.

Today, my daughter continues to have three-month checkups with the oncologist. She is back to doing schoolwork five days a week (via e-learning due to COVID-19). She gets OT two days a week, PT two days a week, and speech therapy one day a week. Her speech is constantly improving. Her handwriting is almost back to her baseline from before her surgery. She is still weak; she can't shoot a basketball into the hoop yet. We continue to help her strengthen and grow in the right direction.

During this whole process of surgery, radiation, and chemotherapy, my daughter lost about eighteen pounds. She has now gained eight pounds back, and we are eight months out from chemotherapy. She says, "Food tastes much better again." Youth is definitely to her advantage.

When chemotherapy was finished, our daughter got to pick a Bear Hug through the Bear Necessities Pediatric Cancer Foundation. A Bear Hug is a custom experience that pediatric cancer patients in the Chicago area can design and enjoy with the help of the foundation. She chose to go to New York City. We stayed at the Langham Hotel on Fifth Avenue. We went to see the Statue of Liberty and ate at a famous restaurant called the Sugar Factory. We were very glad to be there. We explored New York City and had a terrific time. Our daughter picked an amazing trip.

As of this writing, it has been eight months since my daughter had any sort of medical treatment, and she can walk up to 460 feet on her own. She was using supra malleolar orthotics (SMOs) inside her shoes, which are plastic ankle supports. She only needed them for a couple of months, until she felt independent. She still uses a posterior walker for distance and when she gets tired. She is now seeing balance and neurological therapists.

She has amazing ideas about how to prosper and get back to 100 percent. In two visits, she has focused on grasping her body with her mind and making her body feel like it is properly oriented in space.

I believe that one year from now, my daughter will be 100 percent back to the way she was before the day I learned she had something horrific. She is a fighter, a warrior, and a champion. I know she will continue to dedicate as much effort as she has to in order to regain her previous baseline.

We still don't know why this happened to us or her. What we do believe is that there is a reason that will become clear in the future why God picked her and our family to go on this journey.

Thank you, Coach, for your time and dedication

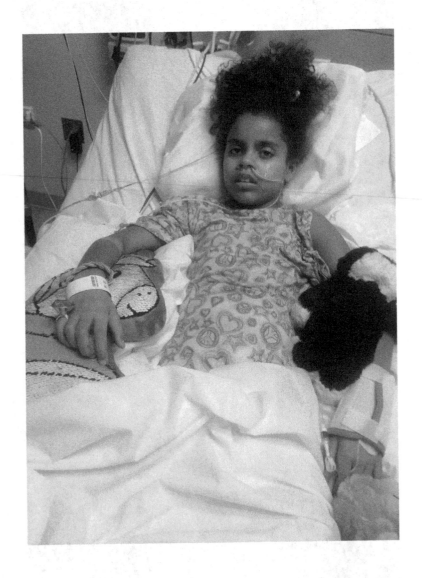

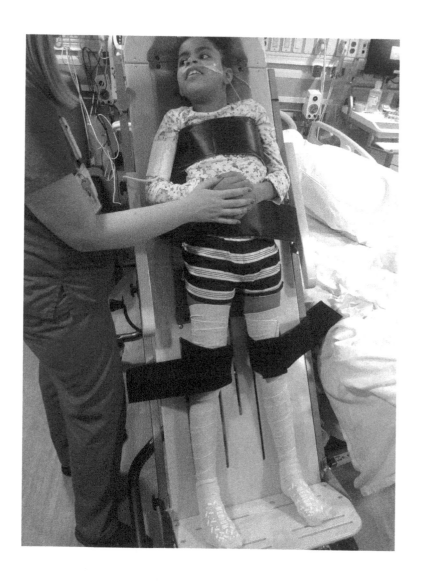

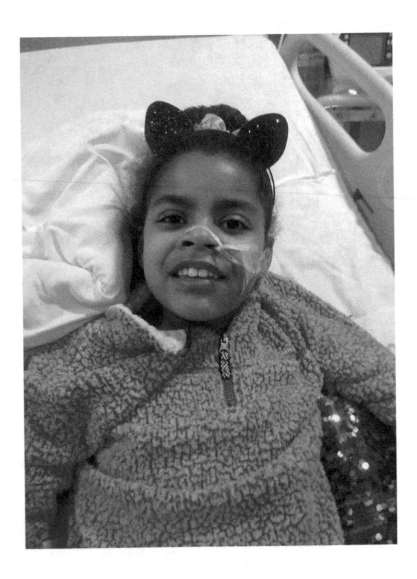

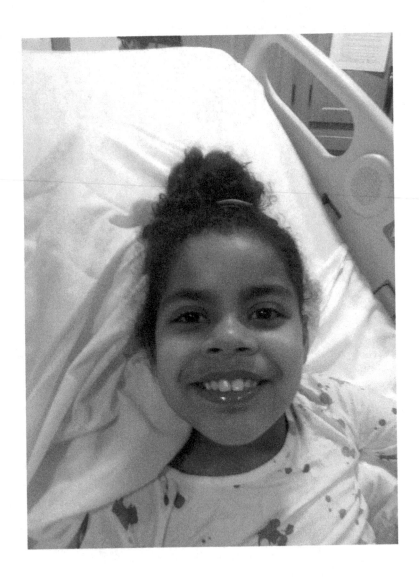

PATIENT SCHEDULE

KARIINA A WILLIAMS   Room 3308

Thursday
02/28/2019

Time	Dur	Activity	Provider
6:00am 6:30am		NURSING CARE	
06:15am 15		NURSE DAILY WEIGHTS	3 WEST NURSING
06:30am 180		OUTAPPOINTMENT	OUTSIDE APPOINTMENT
07:00am 30		BREAKFAST	MEALS FOR INPATIENTS
10:00am 60		PT CASTING	PEDIATRIC REHAB TECH
11:30am 30		OCCUPATIONAL THERAPY - 30 MINS	LAUREN S OT
12:00pm 60		LUNCH - PLEASE COMPLETE MENU	MEALS FOR INPATIENTS
12:00pm 30		SPEECH THERAPY 30 MIN	RIMA BIRUTIS SLP
12:30pm 60		REST PERIOD	NURSING BLOCK
01:30pm 30		SPEECH THERAPY 30 MIN	RIMA BIRUTIS SLP
02:00pm 30		PHYSICAL THERAPY 30MIN	MORGAN C PT
02:30pm 30		OCCUPATIONAL THERAPY - 30 MINS	LAUREN S OT
05:30pm 60		DINNER	MEALS FOR INPATIENTS

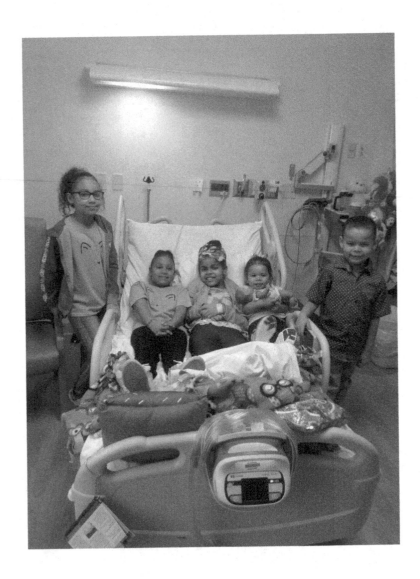

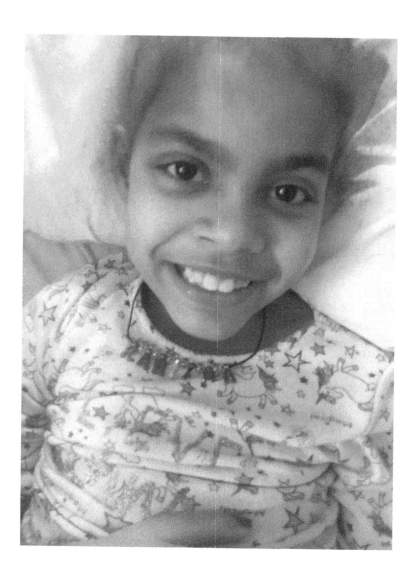

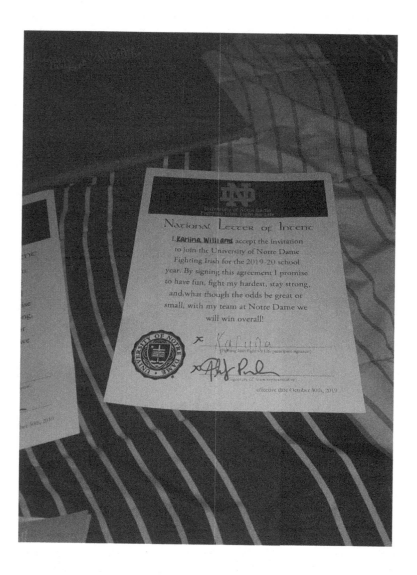

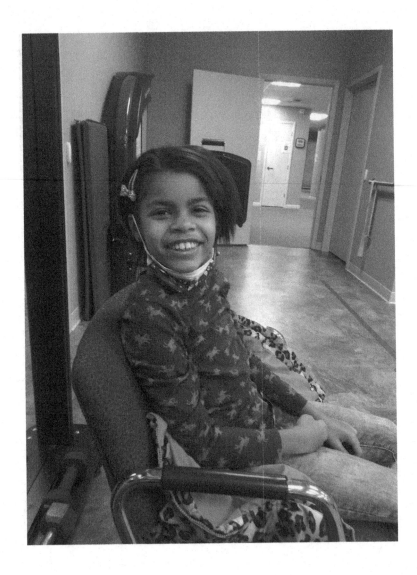

Printed in the United States
by Baker & Taylor Publisher Services